Along the Vine

A Collection of Christian Poems

JAN MILLER

WestBow Press books may be ordered through booksellers or by contacting:

WestBow Press
A Division of Thomas Nelson & Zondervan
1663 Liberty Drive
Bloomington, IN 47403
www.westbowpress.com
844-714-3454

Because of the dynamic nature of the Internet, any web addresses or links contained in this book may have changed since publication and may no longer be valid. The views expressed in this work are solely those of the author and do not necessarily reflect the views of the publisher, and the publisher hereby disclaims any responsibility for them.

Any people depicted in stock imagery provided by Getty Images are models, and such images are being used for illustrative purposes only.
Certain stock imagery © Getty Images.

Scripture quotations marked NKJV are taken from the New King James Version®. Copyright © 1982 by Thomas Nelson. Used by permission. All rights reserved.

Scripture quotations marked KJV are taken from the King James Version.

ISBN: 978-1-6642-7373-3 (sc)
ISBN: 978-1-6642-7374-0 (e)

Library of Congress Control Number: 2022913678

Print information available on the last page.

WestBow Press rev. date: 07/29/2022

WESTBOW
PRESS®
A DIVISION OF THOMAS NELSON
& ZONDERVAN

Along the Vine

A call to arms is the battle cry heard from up above, we are enlisted in a Royal army, we walk in great power, always speaking with words of love. Wherever the Lord will have us to go and whatever He will have us to say or do, our position is firmly in Christ, no, we shall not be moved. Continuing on with the great I AM, each soldier will do His good work, ready to stand on the battlefield, Word in hand. Equipped for conflict, rigorously approved, an unyielding declaration so states, no, we shall not be moved. By the Word of the Lord victory is near, thus, let us move boldly ahead with armor and all to heed the dear Saviour's call. For we shall not waiver and neither shall fall. Through the day and through the night we must march speedily, doing what is right; no, we shall not be moved, this is our plight. A clear sighted troop that we are, remaining in His presence, never to depart. To take the high ground by not giving one inch, a highly skilled infantry will plant the Crimson stained flag in order and in Truth; so, in Christ, no, we shall not be moved. Yet in all these things we are more than conquerors through him who loved us, having passed through Calvary's path and having learned to wholly trust. Christ made the ultimate sacrifice with the shedding of His blood, where death's tight hold was broken, and in triumph He stood. But thanks be to God, which giveth us the victory through our Lord Jesus Christ; for He has paid our sin debt and purchased eternal life. So, hoist the victory banner, the contest has been won; it was God's perfect ground plan through Jesus, His only begotten Son. It is with a shout and great acclaim, no, we shall not be moved in Jesus name.

Romans 8:37 NKJV
1 Corinthians 15:57 KJV

TREES BELOW
THE SON

To the North, South, East and West, the fields are barren, for many skilled laborers shall assume their duties, thus, go to work on the Landowner's behalf, the Rose of Sharon. Planting season is here, undoubtedly, fair weather will not last long; each worker must seek His face continually in order to surely finish strong. The fallow ground is broken up receiving the heavenly seed; this task is far more than completing just only a good deed. While tilling the soil, we are to watch the sizes of the rows, they require to be deep and wide, in an effort to harvest the most amount of souls. The Overseer is All Wise, instructing field hands to be quick to fertilize; these trees will bear fruit of all kinds, take heed, do not waste any valuable, nor precious time. Living Water causes them to thrive, with proper care, they will live on, never to die. An orchard of a vast and plenteous supply, for They that sow in tears shall reap in joy; herein, is our cry. Hoeing keeps every tree from being overtaken, through the blood of Jesus and holding fast to His Word, we shall not be shaken. This Grade A Yield is of the Root of David flourishing in due season, it will not spoil, which has been decidedly reasoned. We are now at day's end, to eat the fruit of your labor, the Lion's share take in.

Psalm 126:5 KJV
Psalm 128:2 NIV

With the morning tide our anointed vessels embark on a treacherous voyage to a distant land. The Lord Jesus Christ, our Admiral, is in command. We are a massive fleet on a mission whose course has been charted with perfect precision. The Compass inevitably reads a true north; for He is a Man of War, guaranteeing safe passage to Heaven's misty home shore. The Master fisherman says, Follow Me, and I will make you become fishers of men, cast your nets wide, bringing them up and in; be mindful not to fall, therein. Through the looking glass, God's eyes have seen an enormous team of fish, we as His workmen must carefully glean. A harbor awaits for the bountiful crop, it's all hands on deck, thus, full speed ahead, never hesitating nor coming to a stop. Our Lord is not asleep at the wheel, but steering intently with all encompassing skills. Through a great number of riptides and stormy gales our Captain has held the lines and raised the sails. Jesus declares, Peace Be Still, all storms subside; we are now in still waters, sailing at the evening tide. On the horizon there is a beacon of light guiding us in, this Royal navy is by and by at journey's end. Our Commander announces to drop anchor at this dock, his children are home, a most blessed and glorious flock.

Mark 1:17 NKJV
Mark 4:39 KJV

Lookin' in that eastern sky, For the Lord himself shall descend from heaven with a shout, our Deliverer has so come, the time is about. There will be a meeting in the air such as none have ever seen, we shall see Jesus Christ, who is Lord of lords and King of kings. He has prepared the way for His Bride, spotless and pure, for we must be on ready, steady and sure. To ascend to a city, fair and bright, I will walk those streets of gold once again, including great splendor and many people, therein. On heaven's glorious banks we shall stand with family and friends, walking with our sweet Saviour, hearing His marvelous plans. God's chosen by grace, thereupon, the crystal river exceedingly bright, what a time of sweet fellowship, joy and much delight. It is with rejoicing each jubilant heart will resound, we will see Jesus when the trumpet sounds. This home in glory very soon awaits, we shall be in one accord, for we shall be with Jesus, our dear, sweet Saviour and Lord.

1 Thessalonians 4:16 KJV

At the given and appointed time, God opened a window of grace, a glorious light shone forth towards all of mankind; for we were written on the table of God's heart and we were, as well, on His mind. The plan of salvation had long been established within the portals of glory, providing the world with its grandest and most important story. Our Father's love came streaming down, sending a Saviour who would ransom our debt of sin, so that we could go free to walk in newness of life, yes, and amen. Upon those who will believe on Jesus and what He has done at the Cross, God bestows a crown of life; we are saved through grace by faith because of Christ's once and for all, atoning blood sacrifice. While our Creator looked through a window of grace from above, His view was absolute, one of love, for His greatest creation, wanting none to suffer eternal damnation. God's window of grace, Jesus, His Son, reflects His heart and character; so shall we be with Him forevermore, the exciting and final chapter.

IN HIS HANDS

The Good Shepherd softly speaks, I AM here as He guides me along the way, listening with an ever present ear. In His hands I am kept with great and mighty power, in every second of every hour. Angelic hosts have been sanctioned, ministering heaven-sent aid in my timely preservation. For Jesus shall be glorified by many testimonies that are truly miraculous and, indeed, well telling. I must give witness to the strength of His nail scarred hands where Calvary's blood flowed, having there made us clean, yes, being made whole. To those that will only believe, He gifts with eternal life; He is the Son of the living God, our Lord and Saviour, Jesus Christ. Who is, and who was and who is to come desires only the best, verily, who is all knowing, faithfully keeps me in all of my coming and going. My refuge and my fortress that shall never be moved, I am daily walking with him, abiding in His Truth. These hands are of mercy and of grace, He has removed all sin, imputing His righteousness in its place. Glory to God for all that our Redeemer has done, THE CROSS, whereby death was defeated, and victory was won. One day soon I will touch His hands, to humbly kneel at His feet, thank you, Lord Jesus for holding me in your steady keep.

Psalm 91:2 KJV
Revelation 1:8 NKJV

GLORY BOUND

I am but a pilgrim in a foreign land sojourning in grace and mercy, praying that one day in Jesus' presence I will finally stand. In fields of great plenty and much lack thereof, this migrant laborer is headed for a celestial home way up above. I am bound for glory to touch the face of God and to there walk, where the angels have trod. Through fires, floods, muddy waters, too, I have wandered and traversed a far distance in every part of my wilderness experience. My flight has been stormy, but I will very soon set down to marvel in each of heaven's many blissful sounds. We, having been grafted into the true vine, joy unspeakable, oh, how divine, reaching the mark in fullness of time. With hands lifted high offering worship and praise, we shall sing to God be the glory all of our days. The Master builder has been at work, many will feast at Emmanuel's table and drink of new Wine, in perfect harmony to, therein, find. Breaking the Bread of Life which is Truth and what is right, we have knowledge to walk victoriously, thus, to live in the light. Oh, taste and see that the Lord is good; Blessed is the man who trusts in Him! Grace through faith gains us eternal life at our journey's end. In robes of white and faces all aglow, we shall be with Jesus, to this end, we must go. Done with the good fight of faith, forever clinging to the Cross, His outstretched arms will bring us safely across. Behold the Lamb of God standing over a river that flows beyond the throne, at last to see Jesus and to be at our new home.

John 15:1 NKJV
Psalm 34:8 NKJV

HE REMAINS

But there is a friend that sticks closer than a brother, that proves himself over and over; for He cares for me like no other. When people have quickly fled, the Lord Jesus Christ has kept me in His faithful stead. A loyal friend I could not find, but He is Faithful and True, a firm foundation that always comes through. By His Word, Yes, I have loved you with an everlasting love; He daily loads us with benefits, from a treasury that never runs empty, but is continually on full. The Lord leads me and guides me every step of the way as I go along; He is my strength and my shield, my salvation and my belov'ed sweet song. Because of the Cross we can come boldly to the throne of grace, worshiping before Him, truly seeking His face. That we may obtain mercy and find grace to help in time of need, just go to Jesus and simply BELIEVE. Our Redeemer has been everything to me, willing and able to set all men free. My God is my rock, in whom I take refuge; a promise goes to those who are in Christ that he will never leave you nor forsake you. The Lord Jesus remains through thick or thin; He has washed me and cleansed me with His precious blood, giving forgiveness for my many sins. The Prince of Peace who has dealt wondrously with you; O LORD, You are the portion of my inheritance and my cup, a merciful Saviour who refuses to give up. In the twelfth and final hour, I have undoubtedly seen God's mighty, miracle-working power. Jesus has not failed me, nor turned me to the side; He is coming very soon for His church, a pure and spotless Bride. A faithful friend in Jesus I have found, come to His Cross, where love, grace and mercy do richly abound. He is my God that will never change; He remains, He remains, He remains is the sweet refrain!

Jeremiah 31:3 NKJV
Psalm 68:19 NKJV
Psalm 28:7 NKJV
Hebrews 4:16 NKJV
Psalm 18:2 NIV
Deuteronomy 31:6 NIV

Joel 2:26 NKJV
Psalms 16:5 NKJV
Proverbs 18:24 NKJV
Revelation 19:11 KJV
Ephesians 5:27 WNT
Isaiah 9:6 NIV

Golden gates of promise opened wide, the Gatekeeper goes before me lighting the way; this promised Gift is for service, I will seek Him for it, to earnestly pray. The promise of the Father is reserved for every Christian, each one should stake a great claim for the Mighty Infilling. For in a vision I saw a river of water flowing from above, along with praying hands and a multitude of heavenly doves. As the Holy Spirit descended on Christ like a dove, He is a cherished Gift, one of love. A Comforter and Helper bringing sweet peace, if the Lord needed the Spirit how much more do we? The greatest Gift from God outside salvation that will bring about much change; Gifts of the Spirit can now be obtained. Yes, a special treasure lies in store, hereunder, these untarnished, golden gates, forevermore. And so, He led me to a hollow tree, broken and worn; I realized it was a symbol of me, indeed, forlorn. Climbing through a barbed wire fence to come to this spot, hog pen in view, a wonderful promise would soon be fulfilled, a long, awaited dream come true. As I studied God's message with moss covered bark, looking upward, the Son's reflection made it appear as of pure gold; this was also an emblem of what was being told. The Lord used an old tree to demonstrate His miraculous power, I stood and prayed, receiving at the 3 o'clock hour. The Spirit of God now overflows from within to help bring the Lord's harvest quickly in; a mighty rushing river that can purify and cleanse, even the most wayward and wicked of sins. Thank you, dear God, for granting my request; I will gladly serve you, Lord, and do my very best.

Saviour, Saviour, oh, what a Saviour, lovely and divine, for He is the Bridegroom, and we are His Bride, loved by Him, the apple of His eye. God Almighty and soon coming King, glory hallelujah, let the praises ring. There is victory in Jesus and victory in His Cross, who came for the hurting, the dying and the lost, Immanuel, God with us! I have come to depend on Him, yes, to trust. He is omnipotent and omniscient, being to us a merciful Saviour, for that is why He was sent. Jesus is unchanging, the same yesterday, and today and forever, my sweet Saviour and Lord, unto me, a loving elder Brother. Redeemer and my rock of refuge, oh, what a Saviour, who is Faithful and True.

S-Sweet Saviour and Lord
A-Almighty
V-Victory in Jesus and Victory in His Cross
I-Immanuel, God with us
O-Omnipotent and Omniscient
U-Unchanging, the same yesterday, and today and forever
R- Redeemer, my rock of refuge

Saviour, Saviour, oh, what a Saviour, oh, Saviour divine, who died on Calvary's Cross for all of mankind.

Saviour, Saviour, oh, what a Saviour who came from above, His Words ring clear, Yes, I have loved you with an everlasting love.

Saviour, Saviour, oh, what a Saviour, at His Cross where He made room, our Saviour, our Saviour, who is coming very soon.

Saviour, Saviour, oh, what a Saviour, who didn't turn anyone away, He delivered the outcast and the downtrodden that no one else would take.

Saviour, Saviour, oh, what a Saviour, who has broken the dominion of sin, we no longer have to live in bondage, nor the guilt therein.

Saviour, Saviour, oh, what a Saviour, the lover of my soul, we have victory in Jesus with authority over every stronghold.

Saviour, Saviour, oh, what a Saviour having obtained Eternal Redemption for us, I have learned to lean on Jesus, in Him, will I place my trust.

Saviour, Saviour, oh, what a Saviour of mercy and of grace, my sweet Saviour and Lord will I see, face to face.

Saviour, Saviour, oh, what a Saviour, who has brought me a mighty far way, as He is the potter and we are the clay.

Saviour, Saviour, oh, what a Saviour, who is my joy and my delight, He parts many waters, guiding me, even throughout the night.

Saviour, Saviour, oh, what a Saviour, who has led me through a wilderness with great tenderness and also with sweet songs of deliverance. He's been nothing but good; I wasn't where I should have been, therefore, I never understood. It was a failure on my part, but the Lord would carry me to higher ground, as He brought, too, a fresh new start.

Saviour, Saviour, oh, what a Saviour who thinks of me. When I didn't know where to go or what to do, for He has broken up the deep.

Saviour, Saviour, oh, what a Saviour who is Faithful and True, dear sweet Jesus, oh, how I love you!

Saviour, Saviour, oh, what a Saviour, I have come to depend, He loves me yet and still, to His will, I must bend.

Saviour, Saviour, oh, what a Saviour, sweet Saviour of mine, who, indeed, is very generous and who, indeed, is very kind.

Saviour, Saviour, oh, what a Saviour, who sends gifts and blessings our way, He is the Lord of my life, the author and finisher of our faith.

Saviour, Saviour, oh, what a Saviour, who I believe, for He has done many wonderful things for me.

Saviour, Saviour, oh, what a Saviour who gave me my own star, the Lord opened up the heavens, there giving me what I had asked for. It stands out being very, very bright, easy to distinguish in plain sight. He places it all by itself outside of my window and in my path, too; I am truly amazed at what all He will do. Miracles, signs and wonders, to His Word, He is true.

Saviour, Saviour, oh, what a Saviour, who loves me the best, I have followed after Him and been truly blessed.

Saviour, Saviour, oh, what a Saviour, blessed Redeemer and friend, for it is by grace through faith that will bring and keep us in.

Saviour, Saviour, oh, what a Saviour, El Shaddai, God Almighty, who takes my part, always fighting for me.

Saviour, Saviour, oh, what a Saviour, I love and miss Him so, I want to see Jesus, oh, how I want to go.

Saviour, Saviour, oh, what a Saviour, who is everything to me, I shall be with Jesus, it is with Thee I will be.

Zechariah 2:8 NKJV
Matthew 1:23 NKJV
Hebrews 13:8 NKJV
Psalm 31:2 NIV
Revelation 22:6 KJV
Jeremiah 31:3 NKJV
Hebrews 9:12 KJV
Isaiah 64:8 NIV
Psalm 43:4 NIV
Revelation 19:11 KJV
Hebrews 12:2 NKJV
Acts 2:22 KJV
Ephesians 2:8-9 NKJV

Stay with me oh, Lord Jesus, is my humble plea. Please keep Thy loving hand upon me. If Thy were to go, where would I be? I ask that mercy and grace lead me into your presence so surely I will see, oh, my Lord, just please don't leave me. Please get me home is my fervent plea, oh, how I love you, oh, how I need Thee. I stand firmly within your decree, for it is me you wish to see. In my Master's hands He has kept me, Faithful and True, even in darkness He had a plan to deliver and see me through. Oh, how lovely and wonderful it will be when I shall see you and you shall see me; I am your child, oh, Lord, please remember me. For it is in Thy service I pray to be, oh, dear Lord, just please don't leave me. For it is with you I long to be, my dear precious Saviour have mercy upon me and grant me this, is my heartfelt plea. My Lord God when you see Jesus, you see me, please do not take your eyes off of me; it is with you I long to be, dear Lord Jesus, have mercy upon me. Trials by fire, tried and true, I want to see you, Lord, oh, how I love you! My Jesus, yes, I will see, my dear God, just please don't leave me. I wilt pray, it is my humble plea, my dear Lord it is with Thee I will be.

Revelation 19:11 KJV

TO THE CROSS

The only Gospel I know is Jesus Christ and Him crucified, to the Cross I will go under the healing, crimson flow. To the Cross I have been, where Jesus there did save me from every sin; I must renew my faith daily in His finished work, time and time again. As I go forward pressing through, the Lord gently reminds me of what I need to do, to stay at the foot of the Cross, not to move. The Cross was established from the beginning of time where Jesus would redeem all of mankind. To the Cross I have been where Jesus bore my sin and shame, my eyes are not dim, what He must have gone through has been made plain. The cost was dear as He did it as a man, the love of Jesus, I can't fully understand. Since being born again by virtue of the Cross, a new life has begun, we are now in Christ, God's only begotten Son. The old life is over and washed away, under the blood of Jesus I have been given a bright, new day. Despised and rejected of men, for that is what I have been, but God is greater than every failure and every sin; that was handled at the Cross, I am now a new creation in Him. Because of the Cross, the Holy Spirit can help transform us into the Lord's image, we being made like Christ as a result of His atoning, blood sacrifice. We shall be like Him one day, never to stop learning about God's grace, to always keep in mind the price that He paid. The Lord will have a lot to tell us, indeed, a lot to say. To the Cross where He said, It is finished, having been poured out as a drink offering, thus, completing His Father's business.

Isaiah 53:3 KJV
2 Corinthians 5:17 NKJV
1 John 3:2 NKJV
John 19:30 KJV

The End

Printed in the United States
by Baker & Taylor Publisher Services